AMAZING ANIMAL BODIES

Tails

ANNE ACCARDI

NorwoodHouse Press

Cataloging-in-Publication Data

Names: Accardi, Anne.
Title: Tails / Anne Accardi.
Description: Buffalo, NY : Norwood House Press, 2027. | Series: Amazing animal bodies | Includes glossary and index.
Identifiers: ISBN 9781978579606 (pbk.) | ISBN 9781978579613 (library bound) | ISBN 9781978579620 (ebook)
Subjects: LCSH: Tail--Juvenile literature. | Animals--Juvenile literature.
Classification: LCC QL950.6 A33 2027 | DDC 591.41--dc23

Published in 2027 by
Norwood House Press
2544 Clinton Street
Buffalo, NY 14224

Designer: Rhea Magaro
Editor: Kim Thompson

Photo credits: Cover, p. 1 photomaster/Shutterstock.com; p. 5 Rick McCulley/Shutterstock.com; p. 6 Jan Bures/Shutterstock.com; p. 7 jurra8/Shutterstock.com; p. 9 Andrew Atkinson/Shutterstock.com; p. 10 Kristina Zemskikh/Shutterstock.com; p. 11 Viktoriia Viktorovna/Shutterstock.com; p. 12 Coldy Bank/Shutterstock.com; p. 14 GUDKOV ANDREY/Shutterstock.com; p. 15 SeanScottPhotography/Shutterstock.com; p. 17 spatuletail/Shutterstock.com; p. 18 EcoPrint/Shutterstock.com; p. 20 Wirestock Creators/Shutterstock.com; p. 21 Bildagentur Zoonar GmbH/Shutterstock.com;

Printed in the United States of America

TABLE OF CONTENTS

What Are Tails? 4
Kangaroo Tails 8
Dog Tails 10
Fox Tails 12
Whale Tails 14
Monkey Tails 16
Scorpion Tails 19
Bird Tails 20
Glossary 22
Thinking Questions 23
Index 24
About the Author 24

What Are Tails?

A tail is a body part on an animal's **rear**.

Tails can be long or short.

They can be wide or thin.

Some tails have bones inside.

Some do not.

Most tails bend. They can move around. They can curl up.

Kangaroo Tails

Kangaroos use their tails for **balance**. Their tails keep them from tipping over when they jump!

Dog Tails

Tails help dogs **communicate** their feelings. When a dog is happy, it **wags** its tail.

When a dog is scared, it may tuck its tail between its legs.

Fox Tails

Foxes have fluffy tails. If a fox is cold, it can use its tail like a blanket.

Whale Tails

Each side of a whale's tail is called a **fluke**. Flukes look like paddles.

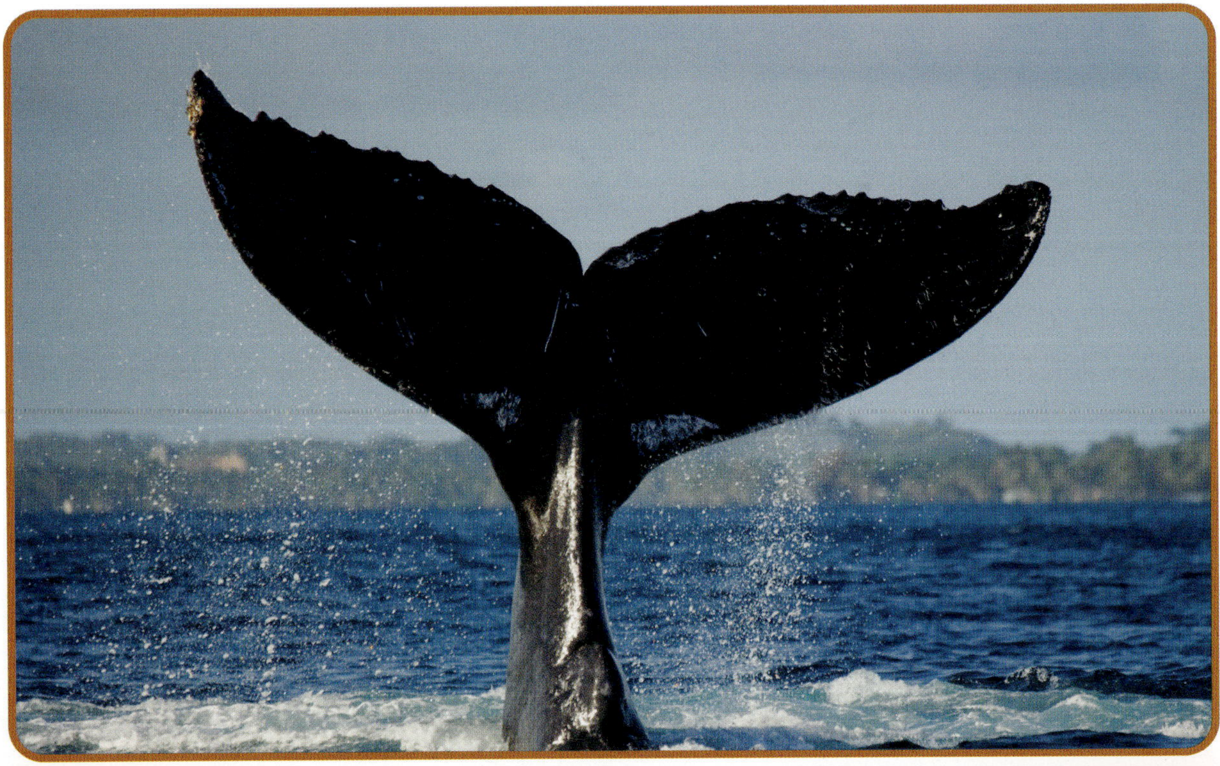

Flukes help whales push powerfully through the water.

Monkey Tails

Tails help monkeys climb and swing in trees. Their tails **grasp** branches, so they do not fall!

Scorpion Tails

A scorpion’s tail has a stinger. It helps the animal **defend** itself.

Bird Tails

Feathers on a bird's tail can spread out or squeeze together.

This helps birds fly, **steer**, and land.

Glossary

balance (BAL-uhns): the ability to stay steady and upright

communicate (kuh-MYOO-ni-kate): to share information and feelings

defend (di-FEND): to protect from danger; to keep enemies away

fluke (flook): one of the two large, flat parts of a whale's tail that move up and down to help the animal swim

grasp (grasp): to grab on to something and hold it tight

rear (reer): the back part of something; an animal's backside or hindquarters

steer (steer): to make something go in a particular direction

wags (wags): moves quickly from side to side

Thinking Questions

1. In what ways can tails move?
2. How can tails help animals communicate?
3. What is special about a scorpion's tail?
4. How does a monkey's tail help it live in the forest?
5. How does a bird's tail help it fly?

Index

balance 8, 16

bones 6

communication 10, 11

defense 19

feathers 20

flukes 14, 15

grasping 16

size 4

About the Author

Anne Accardi is a librarian who loves reading books and learning new things! She lives in Kansas City, Missouri. When she's not writing, Anne enjoys listening to music, exploring nature around the city, and spending time with her family.